Touching and Feeling

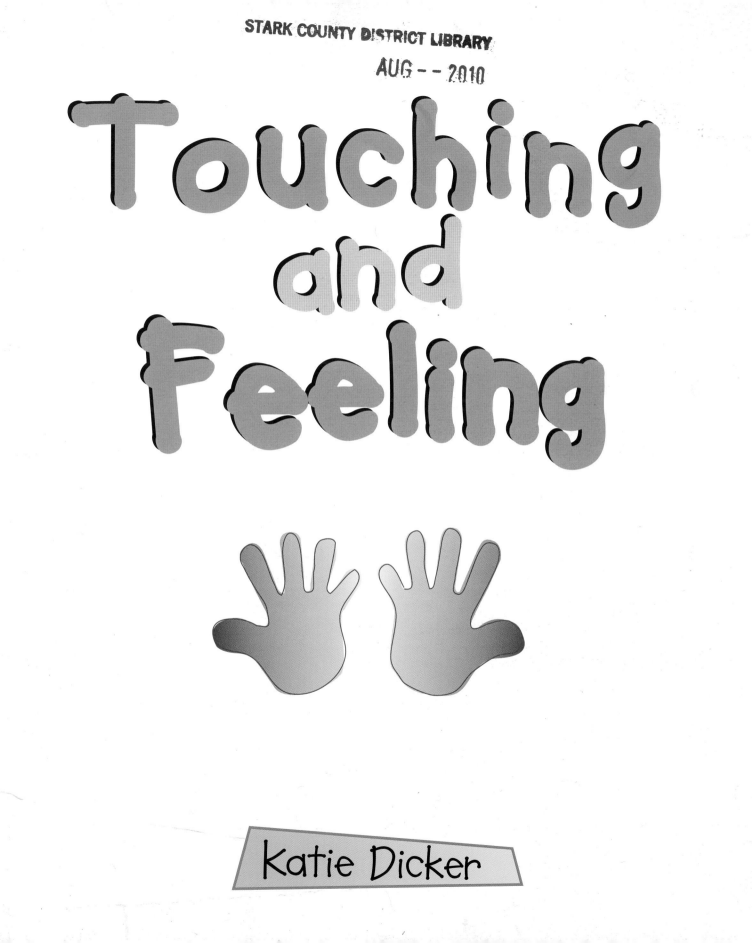

Katie Dicker

Cherrytree Books are distributed in the United States
by Black Rabbit Books, P.O. Box 3263, Mankato, MN 56002

Library of Congress Cataloging-in-Publication Data
Dicker, Katie.
    Touching and feeling / Katie Dicker. -- 1st ed.
        p. cm. -- (Sparklers my senses)
    Includes bibliographical references and index.
    ISBN 978-1-84234-578-8 (hardcover)
    1. Touch--Juvenile literature. I. Title. II. Series.

    QP451.D53 2010
    612.8'8--dc22

                                        2008044115

13-digit ISBN: 9781842345788

First Edition
9 8 7 6 5 4 3 2 1

First published in 2008 by Evans Brothers Ltd.
2A Portman Mansions, Chiltern Street, London W1U 6NR, United Kingdom

Produced for Evans Brothers Limited by
White-Thomson Publishing Ltd

Contents

Use Your Hands!

sssssilky!

Our hands sense the **way** that things **feel**.

4

What do you like to touch with your hands?

tickles!

Rough and Smooth

rough ridges

Shells can *feel* rough and bumpy.

6

This **sand** is **gritty** but **smooth** to **touch**.

Super Skin!

You can *feel* things all over *your* body.

8

What does water feel like on your skin?

9

Hot and Cold

ouch!

The sun has warmed this sand.

It feels very hot!

kapow!

In winter, the snow feels cold and powdery.

Wet and Dry

splash!

Max is clean but soaking wet.

12

blow!

How long does YOUR hair take to feel dry?

Hard and Soft

Hard blocks are good for building.

cuddly!

This bear is soft and squishy.

Slimy and Prickly

slippery!

A snail feels really slimy.

sharp!

Careful! This **cactus** is prickly.

Arts and Crafts

This paint feels

wet and sticky.

steady!

Amit makes his robot tall and strong.

Friends Together

We hold hands to show we're friends.

A hug can *feel* even better!

21

Notes for Adults

Sparklers books are designed to support and extend the learning of young children. The first four titles in the series won a Practical Pre-School Silver Award in the UK. The books' high-interest subjects broaden young readers' knowledge and interests, making them ideal teaching tools as well.

Themed titles
Touching and Feeling is one of four **Senses** titles that explore the five senses of sight, touch, smell, taste, and sound. The other titles are:

Seeing **Hearing** **Tasting and Smelling**

Areas of learning
Each **Senses** title introduces educational concepts (such as personal development, literacy, and observational skills) with subtlety and care. Children increase their knowledge and understanding of the world while developing their creativity.

Making the most of reading time
When reading with younger children, take time to explore the pictures together. Ask children to find, identify, count, or describe different objects. Point out colors and textures. Allow quiet spaces in your reading so that children can ask questions or repeat your words. Try pausing mid-sentence so that children can predict the next word. This sort of participation develops early reading skills.

Follow the words with your finger as you read. The main text is in Infant Sassoon, a clear, friendly font designed for children learning to read and write. The labels and sound effects add fun and give the opportunity to distinguish between levels of communication. Where appropriate, labels, sound effects, or main text may be presented phonically. Encourage children to imitate the sounds.

As you read the book, you can also take the opportunity to talk about the book itself with appropriate vocabulary such as "page," "cover," "back," "front," "photograph," "label," and "page number."

You can also extend children's learning by using the books as a springboard for discussion and further activities. There are a few suggestions on the facing page.

Pages 4–5: Use your Hands!

Fill a dark bag with different items of food, such as fruit, wrapped candies, or nuts and pass the bag around a group of children. Ask each child to touch an item without looking at it, and to describe it to the group. Children could try identifying the feel of objects using different parts of their body, too. Discuss why the hands are so sensitive and which parts of the body do not sense feeling (such as cutting your hair or your nails).

Pages 6–7: Rough and Smooth

Children may enjoy doing "texture rubbings." Collect a variety of shells or leaves for the children to work with. Place each shell or leaf under a sheet of thin paper and gently rub the paper with a dark-colored crayon. An image of the shell/leaf will begin to appear. Ask the children to identify which parts of the shell/leaf are rough and which are smooth.

Pages 8–9: Super Skin!

Children may enjoy collecting different material—such as feathers, pipe cleaners, and wool—and to test what they feel like on their skin. The children could take part in a competition to see who is the least ticklish. Which parts of the body are the most ticklish? Are the children able to tickle themselves?

Pages 10–11: Hot and Cold

Encourage children to explore the feeling of different temperatures. Fill a bowl with iced water, a bowl of tepid water, and a bowl of hand-hot water. Ask the children to put their left hand in the iced water and their right hand in the hand-hot water. Then ask them to put their left hand in the tepid water. What does it feel like? Now add their right hand to the tepid water. What does it feel like this time?

Pages 12–13: Wet and Dry

Collect a sample of different materials or clothes (such as cotton, wool, velvet, denim, and plastic). Encourage children to describe what the materials feel like. Then ask the children to soak the materials in water and hang them up to dry. Check the materials after 2 hours and then again the following day. Which materials take longest to dry? Which materials are waterproof?

Pages 14–15: Hard and Soft

Collect a series of hard or soft blocks of different sizes. Ask the children to arrange the blocks in their order of size, while blindfolded. How many do they get right? Children may also enjoy playing games while blindfolded, such as "braille dominoes," a texture maze, or a simple jigsaw puzzle.

Pages 16–17: Slimy and Prickly

Make a series of texture cards by gluing substances (such as sand, flour, seeds, rice, and glitter) to different cards. You could use materials such as corrugated card and bubble wrap, too. Encourage children to feel the cards while blindfolded and to describe and identify what they are touching.

Pages 18–19: Arts and Crafts

Children may enjoy painting with different tools, to get a sense of different types of textures. Tools could include their finger, a sponge, a toothbrush, a potato, a cork, or a pipe cleaner.

Pages 20–21: Friends Together

Ask children to think about all the ways they have used their sense of touch today. What activities would they have found difficult if they could not feel? Which types of touch helped them to communicate their feelings and emotions?

Index

Picture acknowledgments:
Corbis: 10 (Joson/zefa), 11 (Don Mason), 12 (Tom Stewart), 13 (Roger Ressmeye), 15 (Gulliver/zefa); **Getty Images:** 4 (Anthony Harvie), 6 (Patrick Molnar), 7 (Sakis Papadopoulos), 8-9 (Ariel Skelley), 14 (Andersen Ross), 17 (Martin Ruegner), 19 (Ariel Skelley); **IStockphoto:** 5 (Viorika Prikhodko); **Photolibrary:** 21 (Roy Morsch); **Shutterstock:** 2-3 balls of wool (Angelo Gilardelli), 16 (Marilyn Barbone), 18 (Rob Marmion), 20 (David H. Seymour), 22-23 feathers, 24 feathers (Victoria Alexandrova).